play dead

10 9 8 7 6 5 4 3 2 1

Alice James Books are published by Alice James Poetry Cooperative, Inc.,
an affiliate of the University of Maine at Farmington.

Alice James Books
114 Prescott Street
Farmington, ME 04938
www.alicejamesbooks.org

Library of Congress Cataloging-in-Publication Data

Names: Harris, Francine J., author.
Title: Play dead / Francine J. Harris.
Description: Farmington, ME : Alice James Books, [2016]
Identifiers: LCCN 2015036404 | ISBN 9781938584251 (softcover : acid-free paper)
Subjects: | BISAC: POETRY / American / African American.
Classification: LCC PS3608.A78284 A6 2016 | DDC 811/.6--dc23
LC record available at http://lccn.loc.gov/2015036404

Alice James Books gratefully acknowledges support from individual donors, private foundations,
the University of Maine at Farmington, and the National Endowment for the Arts.

ART WORKS.
arts.gov

Contributions for the production of *play dead* made by: Sarah Gordon and Margot Wizansky

Cover Art: Drawing by Claudio Ethos

play dead

francine j. harris

Alice James Books
FARMINGTON, MAINE
www.alicejamesbooks.org

part one : startle.

part two : blink.

part three : freeze.

acknowledgments

Many thanks to the journals in which the following poems appeared in their original versions:

The McSweeney's Book of Poets Picking Poets (McSweeney's, 2007): "in"
Tran(s)tudies: "pink pigs" first appeared as part of a personal essay
Literary Hub: "in case," "she can sort of see herself dangling her toes in the shot,"
    "suicide note #8: marine snow," and "a horizon of train yards"
Hunger Mountain: "where you could sit up straight"
Bat City Review: "afterwards the boys stand in the kitchen"
Killer Verse: Poems of Murder and Mayhem (Everyman's Library Pocket Poets, 2011):
    "In Rostov, the butcher"
A Gathering of the Tribes: "doubt" originally appeared as "peripheral counts"
Meridian: "Judith and Holofernes"
Sou'wester: "a brief history of scent" and "Kara you wild.andIdon'tknow"
Newfound: "a new fragrance" and "taphophobia"
B O D Y: "suicide note #3"
Heavy Feather Review: "suicide note #4," "suicide note #11" and "Today I watched a
    porn from Japan where girl in a straw, blonde wig"
Southern Indiana Review: "suicide note #10"
Boxcar Poetry Review: "tatterdemalion"
Prairie Schooner: "in the outfield, daydreaming"
Los Angeles Review of Books: "Study after Velazquez's Portrait of Pope Innocent X"
Boston Review: "canvas"
Poetry: "enough food and a mom," "gravity furnace" and "first, take a fistful of hair"
Vinyl Poetry: "how to take down an altar"

I am indebted to the following friends, colleagues, institutions, projects, and programs:

For their generous support in giving me time, resources and funding to write and edit this collection: National Endowment for the Arts, University of Michigan's Helen Zell Writers' Program, Front Street Writers, The MFA Program at Washington University in St. Louis, and *Boston Review*.

For people whose perspective and feedback have been invaluable during the making of this work: Particularly my Alice buddy, Kazim Ali, for his thoughtful critique when the manuscript was still a hot mess and John Casteen for his keen and patient eye on multiple versions and for asking me the hard questions. Much thanks also to Carey Salerno, Lorna Goodison, A. Van Jordan, Laura Kasischke, Keith Taylor, Benjamin Paloff, Major Jackson, and Timothy Donnelly.

To the people who in many ways made the development of this collection possible through their friendship, feedback and professional support: Marcus Wicker, the multitude of Grinders, Cave Canem poets, C. Davida Ingram, Brandon Som, Tamiko Beyer, Nate Marshall, Paula Jane Mendoza, Lisa Wiliams, David Griffith, Justin Phillip Reed, Phillip B. Williams, Jamaal May, Tarfia Faizullah, Airea D. Matthews, Nandi Comer, and all my Detroit poetry people; and the folks who come to readings and make the connection human. As always, this book is in loving memory of Frank and Mary Grace Johnson.

for Lawrence

Nothing you wouldn't know about.

—Gayl Jones
from *Eva's Man*

part one : startle.

in

The body starts a wind when it gets broken into. At night, when the leaves can't sleep
the black bark is one eye open and the snap vine dozes with its thorn in reach.

You come. ready to kill for a seed. a nickel. a splash of sap from a dead tree.
You wear orange. You walk up, skip. You're the big, sad juice. In summer, you knock.
God forbid it roots. puts itself alone between door and the sweat, sweet night.

We don't always think in locks. or iron. We set up house to bring. dim it warm
to want. When the windows won't open, we restless with our noses pressing past the screen.

That's the color of nothing so hot. You bring some buddy to make it like poker,
roulette. You bet. hurl body into stove. You win on how long dead weight would take.
You bash blood with glass from instant coffee. So mornings, she jerks to light.

pink pigs

  - You know they say pigs got a scent for each other.

- Rows and rows of pigs.

  - I can smell you turning the corner before I even see.

- Because everyone wants you for something, and I think that's nice.

  - What can I get you. BlackBall. Plunge. Headache.

- I'm 13 years old.

  - Mescaline. Ropedown. Chain.

- Does it hurt when you do it. Pop it in. Does it hurt much.

  - Ain't nobody gonna' hurt you, baby girl. HighRise. Sunset. Head.

- Does everybody feel good.

  - Feel good around me?

- Waistbent. Swagout. Tall as hell.

  - Trigger Happy. Pocket Change. NiggaNigga.

- You look alive in the leaves.

  - Squeal like a honey. I can smell you now, for sure.

- Let me go change my bloomers.

in case

i.

I carried a clit, in case.
                        in case it wasn't rape.
in case the kiss was your lovely. in case, you suck a sore
bruise, too. in case you were steady. your hand was steady.
in case you could talk. I carried a clit, and a wrist in case—
in case I could rub away seam, and you could rinse hem, and we could
stand upright in tubs, muddy like a ledge. in case you could
hear. me, in case I could pick up both feet
            on command, and carry through beds, and
keep my hair out of houses, in
and out of houses. in case the rooms full of
leaves and nightstands where
the drink is sweet. and a schoolyard out the
window, and in case the flagpoles
were empty. in case I could hear
sheets flap, like
            a punch in the thigh.

ii.

One punches thigh open, another
                        writes script. pens
white gown and white banner and white sheet and white
cover and dove. and white birch. and parchment. and white
cinder and slab brick. white ash of punched cunt, white follicles
ripped.
        and we were not winter. all dark and thick and full of mouth.

iii.

We were not wonder. all dark and thick. our mouths
got us kicked. you ask a princ-
ipal, a counselor, the man in the room. our mouths
got us running, soup water from se-
wers, and gentler weather keeps chicks. our mouths
got us full to black rim. to red blather, to-
ward trouble, a generous flight of stairs. our mouths
got us hissed ridiculous. you ask a sham-
an, his snake of women, his clavicle stick. our mouths
got us our bitter ass whipped, pick our own-
ers, our switches, our licks, our shut up. our shut up. our shut up.

woodshop

nightstands butterfly shelves eyeglass holders dollar signs straight back chairs

In certain spaces, the air is wood. sunk
into a refab factory floor, over a drain painted
white, the hope for its boys painted shut below the overhung pipes.

It rarely breathes.

Their faces, hollow and low. They
sway, they grab one another's fists. The way they
spread and flay like nothing is coming. No
saw, no sanded dust. How often the safety glass, or the rusty
emergency rinse

this place, linger. Her feet

don't touch the floor. Their bodies
hand off space, carved into square
shelf and buffed into corners

unfinished guitars cutting boards carved with snakes windowless cars boat bottoms

...that is not the way the saw should move...
...the whole class wants to make a bed frame. there is plenty of muscle. coats in the back...
...when you pull it, lock it, someone lost a finger once, if it creeks it's normal...
...the gulch gets carved, like the flow of a neck. soft spots in a weak wood...
...here, light can't bend...
...so don't scream like you're drowning. anyway, no one is back here anyway...
...seep. the three stream of wood is like an embankment...
...it runs out there. exit marked, but the light is broke. what if we tell 'em you
can't swim...
...some of the boys skip. excuse me. students. to get away from here. god knows where...
...sure any one of them would be happy to show you. all of them...

...

She is her bits.
She has balsa in a frame, a box, a dowel.
To a drowsing oak, beyond the cinder.
Tinder, mostly. The spinning saw. She parts them
                          heart hangers sundials locker mirrors butter knives
each hour she attends.

please don't trance your rabbit

to groom. There's nothing cute. and not a toy to flip. and won't wind
up. and doesn't kick back to say from the inside, *hit*. say from inside, *terror*.
The bunny is stiff. and from the inside trouble, as if you've never
known numb. nerve to the damage of wooden. nerve to the unfit

arbiter of pose. whose two-by-four and stick, whose brass fist
knuckled, whose gun drawn and sweat at the temple, a bunny
heartache. and fur trapped and mouth rigid like rigor and waiting,
and doesn't do well induced. can't kick you in rib or right the spine

shiver or move.

first, take a fistful of hair

Listen first for anyone. Fill your pockets.
Measure the ditch with a wad of gum. Listen.
Stay still. Break open the gate with your fist.
a back seat to torch. ditch it. You will need
someone, still. but later. from a pay phone. for
the rope. Empty your pockets. Check for wild fur
and the pant. who wad seats. or possums who hiss
under wild shrub. Sharp shooters check the wind.
So measure your mouth. the curve of howl. drool
and its drop against the wooden tiles. Possum
under salt and pine. Screech it. Score the rope
with your teeth. Collect the drool in tin.
Check for rust. Pull out the nails. Wait
for the wood to sag of blood. to good and stalled.
Mount the mouth. slip down. Slide under
sludge, until the caves open and break. and
salt your wounds. and play the black cricket.
and nail on the stars. Run low to ground.
until your hairs unseat. and your cheek
full of shotgun howls. and sags. and
and touches its own blood to light.

in the distance

the forest
and the tree
and the piles of timber
and cords twirled to choke
and a sun pinpoints under magnifying glass, so
        fire ants, who pick up the floor
and take it with them, no flesh left, surgeons
and bones, limbs pout from throat, butterfly
        poison and tumbler bellies
and bees of meat, and you chop and chop
clear that
        sweat felled from the flat flame sky
and oh, and oh
and whatdoyoucall'emnowadays, what with mills
and feller bunchers. So in shifts
and back plates
and the shake of helicopters
and the shake under spinal
and back again
and ravage rooter
and take it through soil
and lift to cage, and shake
and unfetter
and douse, and
and barren, you know,
hollow belly
shell, hard against
bark stripped easy, how quick the

horizon.

startle

The minute you say *want*, the light which was red
is most certainly now, a womb—a thing no one wants to
     stare into, most certainly a thistle, where nothing is safe.
     any corner could be a cement truck. or a gun. Strange
no umbrella prong ever catches the eyeball, no
fisherman's hook ever drawn back too far. The fears we have
     of flames on the skin or bones crushed
     under mallets. Though most accounts suggest some kind of
comfort, considering. The body goes limp, the mind
forgets, the pain isn't what he
     remembers, whose wife bludgeoned
     his skull with machete, only—
                          the strange trail
of blood in his eye when he looks, wondering why
she sees him this way now, what the years
     have done.

sister, foster

i.

I am sitting upright. at the height of your elbow.
You are hidden in green curtains and you want

the back of my hair. the place where it coils
around your knuckle. You position yourself, as

if there were any less clover in the light
through the curtains. It's a strange pattern

across your eyelids. If I were older, I would
reach to shut them. I would say it's okay, we

don't ask. But now your face. Only the shrub
of heavy fabric covering the windows, or paint,

or sorrow in your fingertips, the grip of which
sits me. What girl could ever save

light at the tip of her fingers. I am, your
particular theory. There are no flowers. There is

no hard candy in your lap. But then
the man who brings this heavy lighting would also

bring cut-up dolls and switchblades. That would be
his uniform. I understand this. If I could speak

I would name the doll for you. call it a lily. a lilt.
call it some name other little girls might need. You

and I don't need this. We have the color of stems.
We have the dark of this room. I am so much older

than three. I am your arbiter, here.

ii.

Outside me, this family keeps you.

Your mother stacks church fans in a curio.
Your sisters press another foster girl's hair. The man,

who prefers you call him by name, has the eyes of a mole.
His glasses fatten the kitchen. He laughs at anything

anyone wants. If I were older I would tell you to dream
of cooking him. I would tell you that helps. I would tell

you to start with the eyes, scoop out the furtive sockets
together, and twist in rhythm

the lemon, rub
deep heat peppers under rib, but I am

small. My words are not spoons.
I will spend some years

asking boys to cut fingertips with me.
And they will say

what you would say, now. likely. This yank,
your fists in my hair

iii.

that which might ooze from the throat
of a doll I love. Her skin is leather and thick.

You can see the straw of her scalp.
You can still click her eyes shut and watch her

drip into the ruffles of a sundress.
The tangle, eventually. which dries

to a pine. an imperfect collar of
moss. that we will wear forever. that will bog

your body and keep it with me, the soot of which
tastes of dirt and worm. Now, it's not. where

you sit, still growing over everything, at the nape
of my neck. And though I am small

I have said yes now. And wake
and wake and wake in the blown grass of light.

the cafeteria is also assembly

where the lit footage of lynched boys in verdant
trees fills a screen that snaps and rips

as a department head tries to hold it in place, which frames the rough, green square
of her uniform breasts, her skin stockings, her coiled hair, as a boy

drags a black backpack along the counter, which is also

the lunch counter. Sectioned, and soon the salt stock
gravy will drown debone soaked meat and the smell

of projector, of pressed beef, will spill over

the sound of machines spinning reels
          of the latch on the screen catching and catching in the lukewarm room, the soft

rubber burn of a fan, the teacher turning its old body toward

                    a vent and saying *seriously,* as a girl

                    blows a bright, blue bubble wide and wide, *you have to take this*

                              seriously, and touches
                                        the lit
                              brick wall with an eraser
                                        just as the screen snaps again
                              and flops away from that image

                              and so the powder and chalk
                              hits the painted red brick

                              between the charred boy's toes.

where you could sit up straight

I have walked with half a skull and I have walked
with a blanch shell. I have walked, legs
split hungry, and I have walked too old.
and my body bones around the middle.
and I sling open one eye to the white
whale of you, blowing up spittle and gorge
and chunks of barnacle hunkered
between two ankles where I have
inched close to a dribble, a crawl,
a hunkering over like a fat, black man, white chested,
carrying the fragile egg of us over weighted ice. I have walked
on thick toes, and you never said a word. I have walked
hands out of gloves, I have walked. .
dragged sled with you slumped over in it.
and we have fallen on the ice. we have fallen
with our glass bottles of milk and boiled water
and our hands cut up. I have walked carrying roof siding
and wool bedding and fat. and I have walked carrying nails
between fingers, and I have walked with wood
and enough ocean floor to build you
small rooms where you could sit up straight.
I have walked, and you have watched me go.
you have watched me go and said nothing,
and you have said nothing and sat still, great egg.

rlgir

    -   Black Vein. Thick Whip. Devastation. What you taking so long.

-   Without the bra, I'm all chicken fat.

    -   I don't mind. You always had a little fat on you, since you was little.

-   *Lasso licorice. Yell like yeehaw. Got his back against it. Says the hair is soft. Everything'll change now.*

    -   You look like a fine ass pumpkin.

-   I thought we were pigs.

    -   Oink oink.

-   Oink oink.

    -   The grit in my nails is softer now.

-   How long do you do it for. How do you know when it's done.

    -   Feel like I could pop a balloon.

-   I like big metal balloons. With *Happy Birthday* in gold. Buy me a balloon.

    -   Sheeeeeeeeeeeeit.

lgirlgirlgirlgirlgirlgirlgirlgirlgirlgirlgirlgirlgirlgirlgirlgirlgirlgirlgirlgirlgirlgirlgirlgirl

part two : blink.

lights in the room

The genitals are not clear, of course, though they lay one on another, penis on top of penis, child on top of man. The bed is drowning in crickets and no one moves, which is to suggest union, but nothing clear, and the doors swing wide and wider, and starlights in the room, and they are the same person, which is to say dream on top of dream, clay on top of dirt, and so the closet floors unsweep and the cats rewind a mewl and, off in a distant basement, a goat is trapped in a bad position, which is to say horn over horn and boy over man and this is nothing you can understand without talking it through, though it is something. It is. something

who once pushed a door, saw. and could not
who once shut the door, saw. and owned nothing
who once took the door, saw. and from her
who once lost a door, saw. and before words
who once spoke a door, saw. and beneath lights
who once shrunk the door, saw. and inside the heavy floors
who once grew a door, saw.

and now any body on top of body, genital on top of genital is an amorphous stump, a diaphanous and fat horn of head. and any position is in position. and any bed is in reverse, and has been. has always been. The bull sits on top of the chest, the sun beneath its breast.

the distance between how we learned to talk and hope

at thirteen. under leafless trees.
You are

a puffy, black coat. a gray acrylic on porch,

a dull you step from. Reach your hands
inside the down. and

come to me. sure

with everything you are a red oak living, for one
and also a mile, a city. sprawled

branch like root

system. You are tall as blue ash and
you have your lines.

You like to speak in maps.

This is winter's road. You know a fire. You know
a better way. Your thin mustache and face smoke, familiar. You

talk in *come-back* and *stay-close*.

You ask if I'm cold this way, the way I'm going.
As stall, inside

is dry and warm. Against me push,

dumbly
along the door's iron gate.

in Lebanon, a girl who cries crystals

is hounded until they prove her miracle
fake. Seven quartz a day and eventually no one

believes her. Because no one is raised from the dead

in pattern. Nor does the Madonna
hover inside glass Florida skyscrapers.

People ought to know better. A rain of living fish.
The flames beneath waterfalls. Black birds thicket dead sky

and in an Austrian basement, a woman births her father's children for years

which no one claims a miracle. A woman
in Oklahoma holds up a two-year-old baby girl

to keep her lover from being tasered, which is also not
an act of God. Science won't disprove a cop

hanging from a man's neck in a choke hold. We doubt
footage of alien ships in the sky.

afterwards the boys stand in the kitchen

they all drink beer and adjust themselves.
they all sip swig and make jokes.
inside they all adjust themselves and some stay naked. afterwards
they all stink salt. emit wet foot. they all
adjust themselves and move around like soft dirt planets. they all
adjust themselves in constant fidget.
after they all adjust burners on the stove, they all
amble relieved. the bluff glow of the after.
as they all move the pudge about. they all
after grapple. after bump. they all swill malt liquor. adjust
the knives. they all lick from bagged bottles. they all
inside jokes about swim. about bump and slip. they all
adjust the blinds to open. after they all say
girl smile.

in Rostov, the butcher

has left a mess because (his mouth full of skin), but

    also because the big mother monster again. ever gnawing
    at his war of nipples. Not because fields of grain on fire

    or because the chewing made of bodies he knew when the Ukraine starved.
    not for doctors who helped gouge out the babies to eat—not even for his mother

but for

    his lack of erection, mostly. the inability to lap.
    to quiver the living to a feathery kiss, unless

        he choked her, like. a fist on tube. a wrench on fissure
        when most of them were too young, anyway. the man

            had baby teeth. nothing like the eyes, which

could have torn any gaze from its breast. not like

a land mine, per se, tossing wombs above thrashed field.
        not
a shed of soldier belly spilled like a laughing piss
over exploded uterus. But like the caw

of cud. cutting pink

    organ around organ.
    a body instrument.

the war, itself.

gravity furnace

She wants to set the house on fire,
gas in both hands, gas on the wall.

It'd be like the sea torched from its floor. She'd run like light

from basement windows. or maybe
suck all arms to room ablaze, so housed

in gut piping. the copper hollowed, reaching to a
heated, black rot at bottom. Like ants; maybe she crawl in the dark.

low on the belly maybe she thug out late, lay low
and ink eight walls. lay low like cold, she might

strip bare, black glass. Sometimes strut, sometimes
hide late. She runs from house to ember,

a sum of sink. She breathes through flame
a room of spoons. one

bar brick, one black-eyed room splatter, one torch
spent for each arm, from coal to alley, she heaves

hue of concrete into each limb. A house of blue ring flames
to mimic; someone better run.

doubt

Because you were overweight and wore chains of turquoise
because you were my mother
because you were crazy at the time
because you hadn't, you said, had sex in five years
because you were crazy at the time and because the pallor of your skin
        was changing
because your daughter, my sister, stood head shaking while we held
        your voice on the phone and because your daughter, my sister said you were
        making it all up
because the room didn't move when you came home and no one got you water
because you were crazy at the time and the woman becoming chameleon, skin jade and
        bloated eyes before me was not my mother
because you were white
because it happened four doors down, if it happened, so you said
because I had played with his daughter as a young girl and once as a young girl I caved in
        her stomach with my foot, she sank
because she called him Daddy the way not all little girls get to do
because you wore polyester flowers and because he was thick-moustached and drank dark rum
        at his living room shag rug bar
because your husband didn't kill him
because you wouldn't let us call the police since you were crazy at the time and thought
        they'd take you away, 3 a.m.
because they had taken you away before when you called the police on your husband,
        my father
because you were overweight
because you called home several times that night to report
        you were still o.k. and would be home as soon as he
        let you leave
because your husband didn't kill him
because I couldn't see you over the phone
because over the years no one has said much when you bring it up
because my father didn't kill him
because you were crazy at the time and because as it has happened over the years, I would not
        react the same, react the same, would not react

because we knew his name

because you had been jealous of his wife, her mother, before she left him, the beverly, tall and
        prance, rose-eyed and peppercorn about mahogany tulip mouth, because you
        often accused my father of wanting her

because you cried

because I don't remember you coming home that night

because Daddy didn't kill
        any of them

because it was easier not to.

Judith and Holofernes

                A meat
            to divide and a throat to be mine in its sleek
                    body, brutal, drunken skin
whose touch I take,   too, with his own sword, roar with you
            again, this night, just between
                    me
            and your severed head.

By now you know the moan is a code
            and the moon has its weep
and you are a tangle of things I elude—
            a seclusion of swords and whores who beg
                    at the shift of your knee and the set of your chest.

You know the bargain
            the fat settled score, the weight
                    below the ghosts of my Jews
                            who set their sites along your head
                    and shifted pigs inside their pants
                            in daydream of your hanged head
                    and scruff, dragged to bones they stack
                            to take back Israel from you.

                    And by now, the gulp
                            of your neck has licked the thick of my fist
                    with its gargle and wag
                            its ripped kill of jaw, your throat
            imbibed with its own wide open
                    bloody mouth.

By now, you can feel the stain
            of my breasts where you said
                    it would stain, the low-grown night vine
                            loud couch of hip-holding you do

when I come to you firelight and tentside
      to straddle my country around you, and you

know how I breathe
      a brushfire cage in the horses leaving, the light
         we lick between what my God keeps
            and you, king, twirl at your fingertips. The devil leers

Holofernes, as much as we might like
      a thick twine of lips, there is still…

a woman looks at her breasts in the mirror the way

her father would have looked at his chest.
Looking for where the rib, if he were
an evening, then weather would stretch
and light, each eclipse ragged

against night rose. every thump would stereo
stereo. He would touch her
breast the way she would touch
his chest. leaf to pond.

a brief history of scent

In 1984 sex with the boy across the street
                              required baby oil.
              Not just because it was behind
every mother's bathroom mirror, but because,
                                        as he tells you now, all these years later

              I remember I could smell the virgin in you
              before you ever even turned the corner,
                                        which
is bottled now, I think. on some display at Macy's—funneled into a spray
              directly from angora testicle, or wait,
                        maybe that's Whore. At any rate…he says

                        I can still smell your pheromones pricking up
while inside the glow of his floor cabinet television
              the massive pixels of a British commentator
                        are covering protests in Cape Town. But in 1985,

              you could make a boy pull out, or at least hope he did, in other words,
              you would know what a real penis felt like. *I mean,*

              you know, we're just talking here, he says. And this

was before the public schools
              made poor girls carry baby dolls which wet themselves
and spit up. I always wonder if they
              could die, too. *I'm a man now,* he says,
                        I could satisfy a woman. And in 1986

              if a boy got you to suck his thingy, you could still say
it was because he told you it was a lollipop. *I mean I can smell the sweat*
                        off your genitals, but I didn't really want to put it like that. Of course

it's hard to take a man seriously, with google and all, but

in 1987 if he believed a cut-up garbage bag, like a cabbage patch
was a respectful way to catch the blood, well, then *that*
                    —you might let him say—*was all that chemistry talking.*

And in 1988, a lot of people got religion,
            which was a good thing, considering
the rumors by then. And late that summer there was talk
            inside the coney islands about the monkey
            and bad needles from Haiti

in between talking about who got picked up in the ball draft
                    and who was headed south to a big ten
                    or east to the Gulf.

        And by 1989, people were getting sick, but to us it looked
                    a lot like leftover from the flood
        of heroin, which must have made mescaline
            and crack seem like
a good alternative, so
    who knows.

        And by 1990, we were out of high school
            and thinking about other things, I guess.
But I wonder if the boys thought then
            the way he has to think now to make this metaphor for it:

                                It's like, you know, a pig
might smell nasty to us, but then, a male pig will smell a female pig

            in all that funk and mud and shit and you know…
                I mean…it's on, right?
                        and you laugh and ask
if you are the pigs in this scenario. And by 1991

33

they had a name for it. Then
everything changed.
 And maybe that's why, since you're
 just talking and all, counting

 the gray hairs in his heavy, prickly beard
 you decide to ask him if
 he has been tested
 lately.

she can sort of see herself dangling her toes in the shot

where everyone cums fast because they want to go home. The camera man's
stomach is growling and he has the hiccups. The gist of today's shoot is

girl-on-girl in sequins thong with stone-edged stream full of guppies. all
different colors. Some guppies have fins. Some of them look stoned.

Or maybe it's boy-on-girl with sequins collars and graffiti ties. sequins anal beads. sequins
lipstick. This shot will involve a small waterfall. the sound of rushing water. There is

the pan out from a helicopter. Some of the grips help drop buckets of fish food.
Or, maybe it's boy-on-boy and all the boys have beards. not cubs or bears or hotbods. but

bloated potbellies snacked on Pepperidge Farm goldfish which make them burp on retakes.
Or maybe girl-on-boy, but then he washes her feet in the stream.

The director throws down his shot glass. It breaks. *When the fuck
did everyone fall in love,* he says. Fortunately, there's no glass in the stream. There are

minnows under the bottom boy's earlobes. The girl with the whip in a cupless bra
is brushing his wet chest hair, before it dries to a knot.

wounded, the sway it aches

I am wounded and I want the catcall. I want it, heads
hanging out the window bombinating past

ass when I *tra la la* grocery, when I leisure to mailbox.
When I strut cobblestone to make laundromat

ache for it. I want the old wolf whistle. The bench
stoop cubic. a measuring tape with a Pall Mall in his lip doing

the curbside cry. I like it

like windshield wipers all over rain. I'm broke again and I want
to get hitched at the liquor store, looking for
a wheelchair pimp with a blowpop.

The street is empty without 'em. I am

missing the men to dismiss. No one to fight
with, crude dick. Of course, one could argue

the dip in the back starts to feel
dug out.

You walk, they walk. You slide, they slow
mechanic articulate alongside, like windup remote

robotic lean low, and glimmering teeth with whatever

line they can muster in between
sun spots, in speech, they triangulate duos

three-piece, quartersawn, quintet, sextet, octo-
genarian. They stumble if you trip them.

O street serenade, singsonging *ooohdon'tbesomean* in between the clearing

and bus stop, the first holler I get
I might for strip.

buck

I shot when I stalked you. Well, I'd be your hunter if we both
        bathed in piss. and tilt shotguns to a flame rush. forest, for its sticks

of candle lily

        much of it unspoken: like
            a white wax. like what a kid left on your porch step one summer
            under red bark and things a young girl—oh, fuck. imagine:

I'd still lick holes from your bullseye. lash stitch
a deer wound. tick pick the fur and the skin you bound

        at the ace, you. Where we could be by now, all

            parchment and flint in the bark.

Tell me that body of the hunted wouldn't take
to the arrow like iodine. as in, a wound to stab over and over.

        an entry that could stay the night in a stiff. a still with the throat
        of a horse. like a light snuffed and a mouth

you tell like: remember that time we ate all the headlights.
and you shot out the dark while I stood still.

           Oh, the god. a prey. a brutal scene.
               again with the scripts. where the orange flashing

falls from its camouflage and takes tongue to wood.
The smoke of a rifle. waits again

           for the meadow. to kneel in,   a clear shot.

- Little tiny pink, balloons. Little wee baby, balloons. Smaller than the tip of my tongue.

- Big fat balloons, black but see-through.

- Barely. though. really.

- Stretched wide and stumpy over the burnin' sun.

- So small and cute. Little elastic seeds. Tea-teeny, pink and tiny. Stretchy. Chewy. Tied off at the little bitty baby ends. See how many I can hold in my hand.

- You're gonna' break it all.

- Muthafuckers. Trying to get through my fingers. Maybe if I put 'em all in my pants.

- I can see it from my window at night. Wide over the whole, wide neighborhood. All mouth-licking and sore in the cheeks from blowing too hard and fingers raw from tying.

- That's that tiny shit.

- Big hollow, hovering belly-button balloon.

a new fragrance

you can't pronounce. Where the lapse in reason is the turn of a musth. breaking up
the bed. sweat. catch at the end of a nightstand. It's in the sweaty flowers. in the linens.
Careful what you sand away from the wood. Careful with the lemons [his unzipper]
his soft place strap. He has turned away and stayed. but mark it against you. market lover.
design wool air. strong against what's left. husk over marble, over leather crush. in washer
bins. in tossed sheets, elastic. the endless glove. briefly soft. cotton [estranged] beyond
collar. underneath seat, dug up. In cushions where he sat, carved. grass rooted in stain
on the floor. awl until it breathes. back it to a dressing room window, to seat a cut away.
It's a buyer's river. long to a vast tweed. gabardine loop around its empty neck. a signature
scruff. nothing to note. nothing to collar, to cuff. A blank, suede mold. a mannequin cheek.

suicide note #3: instructions on the cat

Dear Landlord,

Please open the storm windows so he can look down

        into the yard where a young man practices *tae kwon do.*

           He bends
                like the blades of a helicopter. If I were god

    I would still look.
                    breathe
with no screen.

                Feed him tuna. Pet him often.

     But mostly

let him see

        the boy chop air with his hands.

           Sometimes he sees me
              and I stare at his belt. He knows

    it is salt lapping at the rainwater left over
through the screen. We are so high up.

     Sometimes cats also have

vertigo

spinning below us with

his stick.
a perfect

bell.

suicide note #4: to Kevork

To end with a sense of dignity. to take down one's own mortality. to pencil it in. to blame the vessel that married the mode. to unclay. to make a baby's head out of a helpless body. toothless. to plan for the elastic nature of control. to unsnap.

to put needle to skin, pillow to face, trash can to infant. to annihilate the pain of another. Can one *Kevork* one's self. to snuff light. to trash empty. to whiff a gun. to hang by the tips of floorboards. to bleed at the mouth.

to blot out. as in the smashing of glass with one's own glasses against concrete. to stroll along an intestinal trail. to flatten. to treat ocean as morning beverage. to wish down a plane. to place hands along steering wheel at eighty miles an hour and slip. to admit failure. to stoke a belly lake. to blow fire into the porous canals of temple between nasal cavity and eye socket.

to quit. to leave bus stop after waiting. to leave train station after waiting. to leave airport after waiting. to stab in the barn. to cheat. As a definitive clause, to stop. to wail on until still. to smash what is already shattered. to de-eye, as in a goat. to chasten, as in a virgin on coals. to plummet.

to salvage the remainder, as in posthumous memoir. to affect. to flash, most notably like lightning as in electrical current. cliché, to drown, to slit, to blast into a brain. antiquated. to disembowel the guilty before they are quartered. to cannon the body sweating inside the iron maiden.

to pray. to pray and then to do it anyway. to mush.

suicide note #8: marine snow

I am in the lake, in the center
of the picture, just under the surface.

—Margaret Atwood

The stone would\sink

      the heel, \the stomach, sink

/the throat split

      by crag/by

            barnacle, buoy weight/\by

      eelgrass/baleen. Silt

fill the pores and weighted tongue

      pulley a salt mine. Eyes suck

and sponge/pull at the suds off backs of

      sea turtles and crabs vacuum, and lower

         tangle squid/and lower

    press

            into slime stars—shorn

         in the shred of anglerfish/lower, creviced

shoulder to viperfish, and leaked into __seepage

at the bloodtouch_of_____tubeworm.

Divers try this.

And yet
flight, in the flailing arms, will overshadow the
swallowed light. in the last,

fight

meets nothing at all. not

the blowfish. not the eels. certainly
not the jellyfish, whose rude lash and sting

is still no match.

suicide note #10: wet condoms

Dear Blank,

If I start this off by saying he takes his wet condom when he leaves
then it's more about him, less about the desire for evidence, more about
trust, less about the edge of the mattress and the falling sky. less about
the moment the litany turns to shatter inside the overhead light. Or
the last time I saw my mother. more about a zygote in the toilet
or an infant he and I might have held. less about the neighbor
taking out the trash under my window, less about the burn
in my stomach.

If I keep this story up by saying *I never even see him do it*
then it's more about unrequited desire, less about the silence of all spiders
more about how far a woman would go to trap a man, less about
the hyena's bloody paw in any given trap.   more about
how a man must stay free and less about the patterns on the floor—
how they turn from order to distance, how they trail off to what might turn up
murdered in the hallway. It is more about what anyone wouldn't do to be a mother
less about the old man on the balcony in a coughing fit. It is more about the boundaries
the fences, the walls, and less about this goddamn light through the leaves.
how I don't know the word for that. how there must be a word for that.
It's easy to die. It's the easiest thing we can do.

and if I end this by saying *I looked for it. everywhere.*
then it is more about what I wouldn't do to stay alive
less about wanting to remember someone was inside me.

suicide note #11: at exactly 11:59

hang up the rope.

> Hang up the laundry too. while you're at it.
> If you don't mind
> spot treat
> the underwear.

I mean scrub it.

as a mother might
over the rungs again and again in her maize-colored washtub
with Fels-Naptha,
  her tooth sticking out up over her rotting lip, skin flaking off.

    She always meant
to get dentures.

        I always meant to be bionic
                in superhero underwear.

    I did take off
with a popsicle the color of Mars,
and run in my britches, turning six   times and
                twirling
                toward something

                            tall
                        and strong
                    with a lovely neck.

I did spin and flex in our yard
     under clotheslines
     under green apple trees

          in half   Wonder Woman underwear

               half Hulk.

suicide note #18: sometimes I hanged

lovers because they reeked of rain

    children because they tripped when running

        mothers because   horizon,   for heaven's.

    fathers because of

       volcanic

       whippings

   friends because they've lost at lightning
   friends because they ripe and die

   friends because

   because.

others because the wheat

   and gag.

   all the animals just to make sure.

    myself
when the sun was good and done.

glass house

(outdoors) A trapline and pink bursting like melon from a doe
a glass house hunter and a gas huffer blow
cigar smoke over the deer rack. One with a long neck
has been talking about early methods of trapping. The other
has mouth cancer, snuff pushed deep into his lower lip
watches the belly break up over the line
catches up, damn near swallows, when it trips,
choking, they abandon everything, drop their keys and
reach for the gun butt like it might go limp.

(indoors) Now she's a wife who prays for accidents—
maybe not dead, but maimed, enough
to keep him still for awhile. She takes antlers
from their mounts, something to notice
when he gets back, something to say: *Is everything ok?*
but will come out: *What did you do with*
my thing, my thing on the wall?

(outside) In the backyard, the dog looks like a mistake
the wrong breed for the wrong house, an American pit bull
digging wild, *Like someone forgot to erase him from the glass.*

(inside) If anything, the meat she thaws
doesn't want anymore. So she takes a hammer to it.
between the empty spaces on the wall
and doesn't cover the white carpet underneath.

(outdoors) They used to put a spear under a deadfall,
he says, just to make sure. For such a little thing
you could make a bottleneck. They both know that.
It used to be like that. Nothing knew how to crawl
up a backward slope. Still, they like the sound
of the gunfire, how much more solid it sounds.
than the thing falling out there. on itself.

what love could bear the smell

I'd never heard of a concrete liner.
They opened up the ground. for the concrete liner.
The concrete was set stone

like the smeared lip gloss lipstick they put on her.
Her lips must have started to rot. there was a dry scar.

We'd let her stay in the room on the floor. the lights on in the day.
When I touched her corpse, it sighed. which sounded like her.
She had slumped down on one arm. I was afraid to move it. I thought it might come off.
I knew this didn't make sense. afraid to move her dead arm.

Everyone has a different sigh. We covered her face.

I thought it might fall off.
We kept tripping over her foot.
We uncovered her face. her neck.
She was naked and her lips were draped across the space of her missing tooth.
She always looked kinda' silly with that one missing front tooth,
which I never told her. We covered her face.

At first I didn't want them to come and get her.
We uncovered her face. I could sit her upright forever.
We uncovered her face. the light changed. the smell in the carpet.
We covered her face.

At the funeral home they dug out the mole above her lip.
I wondered how they did that.
Sometimes, when I used to look at it, it looked like a blackhead and I wanted to pop it.
She would have let me. try. if I'd asked.
I asked if they could take out the fake tooth at the end. give her mouth a break.

They said they set it so it froze.

now that the carpet is pulled up

your hair fills the house.

In the sun, in a hairbrush. the damp skin.
and cocoa butter. a splash of baby powder, the oil
of your scalp.

Gray strands. a sugar in spoon gravy. a creek

on June nights. When the minnows dip below
the surface, how it gurgles up from the sand. And you,

meanwhile, smack at mosquitoes
who flit beneath it, along the edges of your neck, between

puffs, as usual—you say, this summer
they're gonna' eat you alive.

part three : freeze.

a [blind] translation of Horace's Ode 1.1 (lines 1-17½)

Master (I wanted to say to you Maestro), and return to you Autumn's edict
oh, and press the idiom and dull décor of the maimed.

Submit, as quoted, the curriculum of pilgrims here, to this Olympic

collage (what mathematical frauds
those eulogies, their rote psalming, their noble
tears for the art of dominion).   wet and dousing.

Hung, sully, sunk, such moving turbulence, the large Question—

Illness, sin's proper conduit for horror.

Quid pro quo dear Libel, you risk arrogance.

Gawdy patients find sacrilege
against Attics, conditions as numb

as demoral, the utmost tribes traipse off to Cyber.

Mortal pawns know our secret mares.
Lucky Icarus flits around African
gods of Mercy, mutates openly and odiously

lauds rural soils…

·

on not knowing the word for *solipsism*

Take the sixth-grade fever, and fire
the sick sheets. shiver and the rain
over tubas on the radio, a bloated lung, if I

                                am not on
the bus to school, then who is

                in those pipelined dartmouth seats, who to
                sling backpacks, and play Atari, and slip paper
                spitballs into straws, who to snap open umbrellas
                to poke at whom, who in the

        bus moving rain over gravel, over pothole, under overpass.
                whose chair pad squeaks, or whose
        wheels spun out, whose brakes to grind, whose muddy

shoes on whose feet, or whose pencil prone with sharp tip. whose

punch, pinch, grope
                        to want. Once we get there, no

one to hide with, no cubbies to huddle in blushing, no crowds to mumble under, no

                        sun to come in first thing
                            and open wide.

apparent death

i.

At night, blue-lit washers leak
laundromat through the white vents.
Chinese takeout trays litter
gutters. Some footprints wet streets'
winter. The paneer at cab
stop fills up bowls cheaper than
the lamb spun on spits. Under

        a high window, it's
             a long drop
                 to a courtyard mattress, a wreck
      from a fire escape, from any
            ladder down, from each
   hour of steam, in city, every
       stopped train. It
       climb steep
                the stairs, knock
    at doors.

             That which answers

             takes leg. to push
             its cloth between
                legs.
             Everywhere
             this is how it announces. Sometimes

                I lie so still and wait
                to see how still, it will take.

ii.

Because the fetid suggestion ranks

       among bedsheets, among mumbling, we thought
       so surmised, so familiar   limpid. as

       nested and flimsy as board, rather
       supine and flank. The position

       against insufflation.

who panicked.

       who withdrew breath. lifted listless
       meat from which dry flesh. who rolled

       against buckram
       and bent whose signature

       to stitch. whose flat, red
       soreness of cheek, or uncoddled

       thick flap between hip. which
       of us mouthed that pity.

       which of us called up the dumb
       digger of any dead, wet ditch to come.

iii.

his breath. against fixed neck. This is the news.
The body quits its nervous shunt. June bugs

do it; possum do it. lie with unparalleled waste
of time passing, nerves in inner ears, dizzy. Blame

the toxins. the shock of fabric. the blank strap
mouth equipped to slack away from rant. Listen

nightly. the quiet rag of rough absence. whose
line is it, whose turn. to fold themselves into lack.

into the uninviting wing of gape open. into
whatever dark, like a door, hangs on this hinge.

what you trapped in a bruise, you left

to swell in buckets, to lower, to seep,
to edge down and knock against the well wall,
to contuse stone, to split skin and suck at,
to water leech. to crawl, or slip away from the surface
to dowse, to dive for as if to coffer
to suction or hunt for level
to seek osmosis. You thought

of center, but you forgot the skin

below the skin
below membrane
below the rub of two square plots
below the thumb berry-blued
below the plundered melon
below the melon garden, pulp smashed and pounded
below the collision of soil, the fall
below the tongue in the soil
below the thump of chest against

the curtain wall.

tatterdemalion

I am sad when I hear the first cupped moan of a woman. It is usually from behind a wall. It is usually in the quiet. It is usually not dark enough. It is as if it were resisting light. as if a rhizome, first coming through the soil. If you needed this space, I wish I could plant it. I wish I could cook it. The light is everywhere. I love our small. I love the grasses I don't want to weed. I like the stung nettle. I like the foxtail and the dandelion and the cocklebur. I know this is rampant. I know the roots getting thick. I love the first cupped thistle in morning. I love the tangle violet. It grows anywhere. Why is this a bad thing. I know where the throat needs sun. I know it must stay young. I wish everything. Maybe I love you small. I love the wild carrot that eats bull thistle. Maybe I am pigweed growing a trunk. Maybe I am grown overnight. What parts of me shake loose dirt. What parts wait until you are bare. My jejune bluegrass, why do I eat your light. There are grasses growing up the shabby fence. All of them fluid blade. We sway. creep easily. What parts of me are wild. What parts storing up for the choke. How do I tell the difference.

I ought to see myself as the noble rider

not the mutt, winged horse. the one whose hoof is off.
the one unmade and hunched bridle. naying
backward. the cockeyed one. Daydream sky

of bitter apple. sucker-punched. the one with a limp.
un-noble mixture happened to stir. Dream
a weave-bobber. the non–

cartographer. the wet-nosed
blind. the knuckled hysteric. the one
knob-kneed. the one *whinny whinny*. the one

pulling left. Here a sister, order's hissy.
Some steer at my back who loves enough
but whose name I forget. I forgot.

and now that hour has light. a weary. a stone.
after George Herbert

At the end of winter, morning
             is just a window. No voice, no
altar to speak. Go

        religious, pull the flesh down, make
a votive. or a gun. or
             a pattern of blistery rain. The year
                              relieves
             and light. and every thing
we own, as body. pull down
to its ground. Pull down

        the vertebrae to stoop and beg. and yet
nothing much to want
                    from the bent spine but its
muted gene, its solace of hours. Like children, or

stone. Hard, the belly. the womb. Hard,
the floor, the stoop. nothing to request. The world

        goes and the spine hushes

away. What handprint takes to handprint
to say its empty song. Not hunted, then

a thing forgot. As it goes, the end of light
is not
        broadcast. or namesake. simple
                              hours
        to fill the palm and hours
        to wash away the rib its rib.

A mercy, if bodies seek bodies to make,

then the season is down here with me

> on its icy knees. familiar friend
> who makes no oath to leave.

> no need to pray for linger, as it always
>   lovely   goes.

the storm took goats

Sometimes, I expect to see it in the doorway

trimming carpet with its teeth,
licking paint from the walls.

At night, I walk the goat on a belt with a silver lash buckle.

I linger at stoplights
to see what she eats.   She eats

heavy staples from phone poles
and metal eyelets from a little boy's shoes.

In parking lots, she eats rust from dented car hoods. She eats
at seat belts shut in the slam
of passenger doors.

She eats

the crusted winter salt in spring
that lingers from protruding pipes. She eats

scrap film and licks the spines
of soggy books.

And then the leash

is empty, catching
on stairs.

in the outfield, daydreaming

The slugs we called caterpillars, some of them larvae, a lot
of them worm, but stuck with good hairs, and stinging at things
like the ball I dropped, their pretty heads urticating, their fat color
diamond, which settled among critters, parting too, like the caterpillar,

the green sea of ants which mounded the outfield and made it horizon. I
forget which pitch, which player at bat, whose team I was on, the boy
with three braids—running and running for it, and how the soft fur
of a body means it's a caterpillar you could hold, and the boy

running from the ball. no, to the ball. because I guess I was
covering my mitt with my shoe, or my knee, or the hairs of my
stomach watching, so the dew was wrapped around my skin, and the grass

incredible and wet as a spring-green blade, kind of like

a cat's weedy tongue, the way the bumps on the tongue move
things into his belly without my
                                        help I lean, on both
                                                    feet then, both
ball and sky roll prickly to the grass, it is
                                        rarely about them. Even

the pitcher is a girl with glasses, who might grow up to send

                                thank you cards. Her name
                                            a season.

Study after Velazquez's Portrait of Pope Innocent X
after Francis Bacon

Under Innocent, my father
holds his stomach and makes a mouth.

The kind of mouth that paints.
The one we know so well. A hole of paints.
a blackout mouth, nearest exit.

He howls as if his stomach. and holds.

I never say *it's the mouth*.

a blown-out bulb to fix or live in. a fallen pivot;

more machine in its hook.

a white seethe, teeth missing.
everywhere electricity is shutting down
and closing over his private parts. He wants to collapse.

He has a pig face atop his own
decorticator.

It's the mouth

as he skins, and drains.

Of course, I know and he knows I know but we both pretend.

He is ugly when he makes this mouth
gums poked out.

dilation, the floor, the cold.
fingers knuckling, so when

he sees me

the painter drags his posture
like a watery skin.

He is shred to bone.

Frame by frame, it would be no match.

On the golden ropes,
the man needs   a stall, a mat,   a place to be sick.

low visibility

You want what runs out through a low visibility.
I want to be burned off by the sun.

We want the same thing. The heat, the road in sun.
a travel stuck mosquito netting. maybe a lucky streak
to suffocate, or at least lust. at best, an intensity that tastes.
lava on a belly where it coils. a quicksand swamp.

We want what rains from fullness. what condensates,
so light breaks and the rays are stuck in a mist, clouded over
and wrecked. What difference is it, the cold
from summer. width. a dense relief.

I have light in my mouth. I hunger you. You want
what comes in drag. a black squirrel in a black tar lane,
fresh from exhaust, hot and July's unearthed steam.
You want to watch it run over. to study the sog.

You want the stink of gristle buried in a muggy weather.
I want the faulty mirage. a life of grass.
we want the same thing. We want their deaths
to break up the sun.

a horizon of train yards

The erotic cannot be felt secondhand.
—Audre Lorde

    i.

widens the violet field between grinning street and woodpile
and steer clear.   There is too much blank backdrop
under plane wings and unhitched semi cab junk.   In the habit of traversable space
fenced-in blocks layer hard ground and stick. There is no shift. no
black earth to sprout vines. The wire-backed grasses
        do little platelet. Whatever can grow, weeds soft. no yellow sprig. Each
trunk fits like base in abandoned palette.

How do boys ruin. How do they sway out in the stump rot, cinder block garden.
    They are picking apart the full bloom of gray petal
    planted since the longest day, the birth of steel.
        It isn't his fault
is it, the brown bag stuffed in him everywhere, his hair
a decibel of rail and tie, since the fullest crib, snatched engine
from the swirl of blue steam rising, neck-bottled
strewn to the rocks. I've said this before.

The switch renders that figure, and so I woman in it

        get down on my belly and snake the ballast, like
the shingle of a train whistle. A slow rattle lull, the weight
of crossing guard bells   clanging in grave, slower

once the leg I slog, falls from beat.
    Now it hunkers horizon in flints.   Tell them
it's the rest of this life.

ii.

I pick the channel and change it until I can find two men stuffing both dicks into
one vagina

             who would eat off that plate. Which of them would lick
his mouth of dinner parsley. Which would suck the rain from cleat
which would fill each other's arms with all the testicles, all the prominence
with their inverted trapezoid hip. Couldn't we reframe and take each other by waist
        like heavy books, spines swapped. Each boy hefted, falling to either side.

iii.

The train stays solid as the lights swing across belly and slice
air. The back of spine cools the black gravel. I am curved

like the switch. The scissor crossing each frog at night, hard
along a knobbed fence. Each hour is first like splinter, then burnt. Then

a hundred hands I take at the low gate.

        I pore over each scalp and neck, licking for coal.
                                        All of them move.
        the bulkhead is rattling gold container. the piggyback
        hunting ass in the air.   If I were a man calling at the edge of a gondola

        I would latch on. each tempo a knuckler. each tint
        a container, each coupler. Who in our overheating   did the boys want
                                        against the livestock slats.

iv.

All this talk of hinge

the hump inherent. A slow bell moves through gantry
each time the gate arm lifts.

today I watched a porn from Japan where a girl in a straw, blonde wig

is picked up in an unmarked minivan, taken to a warehouse, tied up
and vibrated. Severely vibrated.

Tits out, red underwear, and a gang of men wearing black gloves vibrate her.
      tons of vibrators. long, white, bulbous vibrators from the 80's. big, fathead
      vibrators, the kind you can't get up inside you.

      First two, then four, then six vibrators.
Then a duct-taped machine
      of a gross of vibrators.
a rope of vibrators. They look like

pop mics. They look like
aliens. They look like

potato heads, her body full of vibrators and vibrators
and vibrators. On camera

she passes out. One of them wakes her
with a black, gloved

finger.

the comedian
(a triptych)

I.

the disappearing magician trick

A woman spills her blush on the train tracks and a comedian steps in it.
The porter asks: *Do you know this woman?*

Since she was a magician in her past life, nothing sticks to her shoe.
The comedian says: *Don't we all know this woman?*
Picks up her compact, touches her wrist.

She thinks about cutting the part in her act about women
in too much makeup, where she goes: *If I wanted a pancake, I'd griddle one.* The train

groans and sags like an old steamer. *This is where some of us wish*
we had more lives to spare, she tells her. She tries to take her hand.
She makes the face of a woman who just felt the saw.

Meanwhile, the stagehand complains about how long it takes
to set up for her shitty act: the water tank, the box of handcuffs, the prosthetic halves

of cut-in-half girls. The magician says: *I used to be a comedian in my last life.*

The rabbits were free.

the comedian
(a triptych)

II.

the poet is a mirror image

Why do you need notes to   *sever people?*   she says
                            and the blue ink dyes
      fill   the rusty bathroom sink
the comedian   grabs her toothbrush
                       takes a razor   to her hairbrush
it's five in the morning and   a
            garbage   truck rattles the tiny flat   lipstick
               stains   all over her hairpiece
        You're a real candy-apple   *ferris wheel*, she says.
             stuck   *at the top.*
                      the comedian has
            shows   tonight.   a mirror full of post
     —it notes.   *A*   *poet*   *needs her*
                      tooth
            brush   she says.

the comedian
(a triptych)

III.

love is best buried

A woman is like a coffin, says the comedian … and lets that joke hang
until the low-level fog has risen to the rafters. Until the last *sweep, sweep*
of the janitor who is smoking a generic cigarette. *Your cigarette smells
like embalming fluid,* says the magician. Her sweat drips into her

gray collar. The janitor laughs. Lays down the broom by the table.
Yeah yeah, and your jokes are like the dirge.
The two split a beer and a stogy. They light up the dark.
You know I was an undertaker in my last life, she says.
And the stage is full of boxes fit for bodies.

And a woman in a black and white picture sits on top of a piano. Her lipstick, she thinks:
Daguerreotype Red. The janitor is a pretty fair bartender, too. The comedian
is soaked in her shirt. The magician is sweating profusely. *I knew a woman,*
says the janitor. And pours the back off a fifth of whiskey. Cuts tobacco with a razor

blade. Licks the paper with a little rabbit tongue. Takes the filter from a butt in the ashtray.
I knew a woman, too, says the poet and sits, wiping her sweat.

straw

I've already pieced it out in my head:
there's almost nothing to go back to.
—D.A. Powell

Which girls answer.

  what window, which door.   Who knocks in the empty streets

or stands them up straight with hair draped over their ears, throats open.

    Who blows into their eyelids, articulates

their wrists and pulls the pin from their break glass

        stomachs. They are bomb

      shells, beekeepers

       hobbyhorses.   Their lips

  snap at the wake of window. The sunlight

    roughshod through the vacant house,

sneaks up   dust.   Who thought to bring the girls

      new panties, clean brushes, pressing

combs. Little teacups

         in the middle room. Little

    swept up hair, pushed

        into corners, where light can't get. Where small hush girls

    hide their holes

        from everyone.

                  to see.

taphophobia

Down in dirt under dirt with silk and the dirt
and the pillow dressed and the air slips. And
the legs stiffen and pin. Not a time for mouth,
but still gaped open, muffled up among the
breath   and   its   enclosure.
Not close enough to worm, to beetle, scented
soil   to   a   dropped   lung.   but   encased.
The dung and rat would be better company,
cold plunge, faster. And the hell of rationed
               gasp. O, enough to wake sudden. and suffocate.

               Enough wait to startle a night
                    at the throat, the heavy silk drape
     under hangar of earth, and what done to deserve the dense plates of monoxide
          covering lips
and ringing

against the roof's catch. the claw hysteric as pant and wail, still warm
               but crushed ton below heaped mud on collapsed chest. If only that.

          or air.
               What panic makes. when forced to flail.

canvas

You want to make a painting of a fat woman.

> As if you could render the skin translucent you start at the stomach. Inside its bag, you start to fill in hot-cross pastries and sausage and hot dogs on a stick.

> You stand her upright.

> You brush out a background in vats of all-purpose flour and Swiss milk chocolate bars near the belly button and figure you may dot areas of ambiguity with gummy bears and popcorn chicken. But instead you find yourself stenciling in

> pigs.

> beheaded cocks.

deli meats layered in folds and you try to render them in a way that doesn't look like reams of pink paper. To round out the folds of this gut, you find yourself sketching in a butcher in sunglasses.

He sits below her ribcage.   He has a cleaver in one hand,
      in the other. a slaughterhouse.

> an electrocuted cow. guts on a hook.
> This reminds you of a fishing pole, which you draw down the
> front
> of her belly,
> like a river.
>   Compositionally,
> you add a man holding a beer in one hand and
> (for whatever reason in the other) six tickets to Disney.

You add workers in the slaughterhouse.

You add a nest full of bees.

You add a crate for the bees who fall dead from her left breast.

You try to paint high fructose.

You wind up drawing someone you imagine to be this woman's boss on a landline phone behind vertical blinds behind a cubicle in a small office of white walls.   Her boss is a woman. The face seems locked in a scream beneath a brow that is penciled in to a furl.

You fill in kid after kid after kid with sticky crap on their faces and broken teeth on monkey bars, their raw little mouths and you draft them along her sternum.

You put some of the children near a conveyor belt. This seems problematic, but makes emotional sense. You shade in

someone's

house slippers and someone else's banged-up knee. Now you are drawing traffic lights and pastors and television sets over her breasts. You add a man ripping off the genitals of a baby pig inside the slaughterhouse.

You paint a figure with its dick out.

You thought you would show a Thanksgiving dinner on her pubic mound, but instead wind up painting an African girl child with *kwashiorkor* and you place her on the upper thigh.   You think better of it. You wonder if there are any American children with *kwashiorkor*.

This sends you back to the slaughterhouse.

You draw panoptical offices.

You draw an overseer.

You paint workers laughing with pig on their boots. You sketch a mother trying to use insulin inside the woman's elbow. You try to paint cancer. You don't know how to paint cancer. You settle for IV tubes and a lot of bottles of pills. You don't know how to convey whether or not the pills are working. You add a forest fire. You crosshatch a fistfight. You keep coming back to the slaughterhouse and fill in picket lines and time clocks and more IV tubes and lots of bottles of pills. You line the walls of her forearms with redbreast robins and heavy clouds in a shady sky. You draw a tide and a shore. You use aquarellable pencils to hint at skinny women inside organic grocery stores under her armpits. You draw a farm with a small baby goat roam free. You are running out of room. You fill in her knees with tofu. diet coke on her ankles. You remember how to draw a hummer limo. You do this inside her toes. You feather in plastic surgeons over movie theatres above her kneecaps under pointillist popcorn, soggy with a slick, clear sap. You draw umbrellas inside her hips. You draw broken bicycles along her collar bone. You draw a seashore behind a jail cell behind her eyes. You draw white couples fucking under her chin. You think better of that and paint brown women fucking in the bulge of her neck. You second guess this decision and draw a picture of her holding someone she can't see along the back of her own spine. You draw a horse in a wedding across her bottom lip. You shade it with your finger. You erase the bouquet.

Kara, you wild.andIdontknow

after Kara Walker's *Cut*

who said to younasty. But I won't picksides now. Every coloredblues
believe able. like I'm a milkflower in your sprayshadow. I want to be

so smooth at the tip. hover above a boundary don't (forgetmehear?

what small clapping we'd have done with pinecones, or Iguess thorn
of myrtle pin pricking, or the needles of a loblolly pine. I bet,

I'da dodged you, too. or no. I liked quiet girls. embedded and pressed
in the skirts above two ashen knees. I wet and no one laughing in you.

No one small pigtail lily. pigtrunk. pugs under dampbrown leaves cut
of the summer's ambivalent elbow. run down by dirty boys, and hug

into the tamped down mud. failed like the seed in hunks of hazy mint
melons in necrotic tub garden. Let's go back and trade kindergartens.

mesh wrists together like dumb boys got to. I don't know about you
but they wouldn't take my blood off rounded scissor tips, mighta'

done us some good.

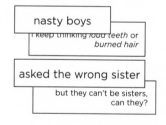

coloredblues?

we'd adone

under

if you liked me

our

lazy

nasty boys

I keep thinking *loud teeth* or
burned hair

asked the wrong sister

but they can't be sisters,
can they?

come back to me.

81

a [blind] translation of Horace's Ode, 1.1 (continued at line 17½)

...my lifelong debt is showing.
Some queenly class has gently handed over their fathers to the homeless.
It is men, isn't it, who poke holes
in uteri to make sure Mr. ManSized never leaves in one piece.

It's the demise of the dead sperm—spurned and undone
swimming still in its holy water.
Multitudes castrated like this and in our microscopic tubes
permanent song bellows along
like motherhood

when it is hated.

Manet under a crown of Ivy
grows cold
unable to document the smallest conjugation. no deep voiced note
no opened wheeze to bring on blue spring and its loyalties,
alone and ruptured,
the painter apes Mars in plague.

Our doctors hydrate the primal lobes
against their arrogant air, the air upon which our names lick the men closer

Nymphatically raises night to Satyr's choir
in a music of hospitals, if never troubled
Euthanasia lives without Fear of Song.

Women love refuge and tender it with a bourbon made to re-open arms.

When and if we write trouble to a bone,
it will chalk your sublime walls with a feral
fever.

enough food and a mom

The dad. body has just enough gravy on his plate to sop up one piece of bread.
So, enough for one supper, says the mom. She comes back to him, says
don't argue with mom, you're a ghost. There's enough water around to drown a cob
in its husk. in a dad. He puts up weather stripping all night. to keep out the mom. He says

I should have cooked for you more. She thinks she could make her own insulin.
to keep herself from going into dad.

She says I should have married a ghost. says: You have a little
raisin on your lip. a little. The mom says stop all that quiet, it's foolish. Come on
now, dad. come to ghost. says the ghost.

I won't even warn the mom. I won't even flinch if the ghost tries to hold her mom. After all,
a good séance starts with enough food and a mom. The ghost with a biscuit in meat. The
mom with the smell of cracked dad. sucked out of oxygen. The mom is
a smell of wrecked vines.

                    You, the dad. with no teeth. And no, (the mom)
is a garden full of ghost. No. says the dad: lost in ashes.

No city is complete. its own worst ghost. who can't even remember the ghost
now, the ghost says: All your selves know, now. They ghost
like the bushel of a snowflower.

Everyone is dead. now. says, the ghost. The mom is a yard of blackening petals.

At night, I have really long dads. Without the ghosts, I wake in a puddle of ghost.
But you'll be mom one day. to know I am alive. We are all sappy dad, aren't
we. Tell the ghost, it's ok. Let the bodies lie ghost for awhile.

I mom of you. I mom of you a lot.

how to take down an altar

First, remove your Mary. Take the chains from her neck.
Then smack out the candles with a pillow. Stack the books

      under Paul in boxes. Lift up
      the snakes. Uncover the faces. Take

            the incense dust in both hands and cross Barbara.
            Unhinge Jesus carefully, at each panel. Move

                the Angels by their buttocks, not their wings.
                Unplug Magdalene. Take away the black gauze

                    from the face of Judas. Pull the river foam
                    below the roses, lay it under both Moses.

                        Wrap Adam and Eve
                        in light citrus and borax. Make a clay paste

                            to preserve the face of God. Bury the
                            cigarettes. the apple peels. the meat.

rlgir

-     One day when we grown, you should come and fix my electricity.

- Am I big in you that way.

  - You take my shoulders and face me to the street.

- Babies in the street dodging cars.

  - See. All over there on the side of the house. Ivyweed. Passionflower. Vine.

- Rosebush. tree bark. coal. Do it hurt? Still?

  - Cabbage root. lady slipper. trough.

lgirlgirlgirlgirlgirlgirlgirlgirlgirlgirlgirlgirlgirlgirlgirlgirlgirlgirlgirlgirlgirlgirl

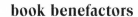

book benefactors

Alice James Books wishes to thank the following individuals who generously contributed toward the publication of *play dead*:

William Epes

For more information about AJB's book benefactor program, contact us via phone or email, or visit alicejamesbooks.org to see a list of forthcoming titles.

Recent Titles from Alice James Books

Thief in the Interior, Phillip B. Williams
Second Empire, Richie Hofmann
Drought-Adapted Vine, Donald Revell
Refuge/es, Michael Broek
O'Nights, Cecily Parks
Yearling, Lo Kwa Mei-en
Sand Opera, Philip Metres
Devil, Dear, Mary Ann McFadden
Eros Is More, Juan Antonio González Iglesias, Translated by Curtis Bauer
Mad Honey Symposium, Sally Wen Mao
Split, Cathy Linh Che
Money Money Money | Water Water Water, Jane Mead
Orphan, Jan Heller Levi
Hum, Jamaal May
Viral, Suzanne Parker
We Come Elemental, Tamiko Beyer
Obscenely Yours, Angelo Nikolopoulos
Mezzanines, Matthew Olzmann
Lit from Inside: 40 Years of Poetry from Alice James Books, Edited by Anne Marie
Macari and Carey Salerno
Black Crow Dress, Roxane Beth Johnson
Dark Elderberry Branch: Poems of Marina Tsvetaeva, A Reading by Ilya Kaminsky and
Jean Valentine
Tantivy, Donald Revell
Murder Ballad, Jane Springer
Sudden Dog, Matthew Pennock
Western Practice, Stephen Motika
me and Nina, Monica A. Hand
Hagar Before the Occupation | Hagar After the Occupation, Amal al-Jubouri
Pier, Janine Oshiro
Heart First into the Forest, Stacy Gnall
This Strange Land, Shara McCallum
lie down too, Lesle Lewis
Panic, Laura McCullough
Milk Dress, Nicole Cooley
Parable of Hide and Seek, Chad Sweeney
Shahid Reads His Own Palm, Reginald Dwayne Betts

Alice James Books has been publishing poetry since 1973. The press was founded in Boston, Massachusetts as a cooperative wherein authors performed the day-to-day undertakings of the press. This collaborative element remains viable even today, as authors who publish with the press are also invited to become members of the editorial board and participate in editorial decisions at the press. The editorial board selects manuscripts for publication via the press's annual, national competition, the Alice James Award. Alice James Books seeks to support women writers and was named for Alice James, sister to William and Henry, whose extraordinary gift for writing went unrecognized during her lifetime.

Printed by McNaughton & Gunn